# A Navy Soldier on Omaha Beach

A Personal Account of the D-Day and World War II Experiences of Gilbert H. Dube, USN, 7th Naval Beach Battalion, Company B-6

Alan C. Dube

The memorial to the 6th Engineer Special Brigade above Omaha Beach

***In memory of my dad, and to all who* served *and sacrificed for our country during World War II. Thank you. You are indeed the greatest generation.***

Alan C. Dube
August, 2005

He stood over the grave of his fallen friend, and the moment overwhelmed him. I rarely saw my father cry when I was growing up – perhaps here and there when he was in the depths of an alcohol-induced depression. This was very different. In the bright, sober sunshine of a clear blue day at the American Cemetery at Colleville-sur-Mer, which overlooks Omaha Beach in Normandy, France, my father started to sob. The images of what he had seen on June 6,1944, came rushing back to him. The memories of a lost friend, and thoughts of a life cut tragically short, were just too much to bear. It was June 7, 1999, and more than fifty-five years after my father had stepped onto the shores of Omaha Beach, and stepped through the gates of hell. This was his first time back to the area since the D-Day invasion, and while there was great joy and merriment during the trip, there were also some haunting recollections to confront.

Gilbert Henry Dube, the son of Henry Dube and Odile Drapeau, was born in Lisbon, Maine, on May 11, 1925. The son of French-Canadian immigrants, and a member of a large family (four boys and six girls), Gilbert grew up in the rough and tumble mill town of Lewiston, Maine, during the Great Depression. A first-generation American, he spoke both English and French out of necessity, attended local schools, and worked at a job in the shoe industry – which was the lifeblood of Lewiston and its large immigrant community. My dad spent much of his free time in the company of colorful and accomplished boxers such as Al "Shiner" Couture and Maurice "Lefty" Lachance.

Then December 7, 1941, changed everything as the United States vaulted into World War II. Gilbert answered the call, enlisting in the Navy late in 1942.

*"All my buddies were joining up, so I did too. I was the only one left around.* (11,8) *I enlisted in Lewiston ...with parental consent because I was only 17."* (4, 1)

After a physical examination in Portland, Maine, my father boarded a train for basic training in Newport, Rhode Island. He wasn't in boot camp for more than three weeks when he broke his leg above the ankle while at the rifle range waiting for his turn to fire his weapon; his leg got caught in between two benches when he was carousing with another recruit, and it snapped.

*"I was in a bit of pain. They took me by ambulance to the Newport Naval Hospital where they set my leg after the swelling went down. I spent a few months hobbling around in my cast with a walking brace on the bottom."* (4, 3)

As a result, Gilbert had to start basic training all over again. He engaged in light duty for a few weeks until his leg completely healed, and then assumed full duties. While my father was on a smoking break with some of his cohorts one day, the chief boxing instructor came up to him, asking if he would volunteer for the camp boxing team. Even though he was smaller in stature (at 5'3" and 140 lbs.) than many of the other men in camp, he gladly accepted.

My dad then spent a lot of time in the gym, listening to lengthy discussions on how to jab, feint, and protect oneself. He watched as the chief instructor shadow boxed; moving about, punching aimlessly in the air, and doing some fancy footwork. After some practice bouts, Gilbert paired off with one of the assistant instructors, who was slightly taller and heavier than he was, for a real boxing match. What the instructor did not know was that my father had spent many hours in the gym before joining the Navy, watching his famous boxing friends spar and practice; he was often given tips and pointers by his buddies. Now he would put some of that advice to good use, or so he thought.

*"I was a little leery going in against such a guy. Come my turn I laced on those big gloves we called 'pillows,' which weighed 16 ounces. We started moving around, not accomplishing too much. He used mostly soft jabs, not wanting to hurt me. Then I made a little move that I should have avoided. I feinted with my right shoulder like I was going to deliver a right hand, and then quickly threw a left hook. I hit him flush on the jaw. [The instructor] backed off a few steps with a surprised look on his face, thinking 'where in the hell did you pick up that little trick.'"* (4, 5)

The instructor then proceeded to beat the tar out of my dad, hitting him with some hard body and head shots. Gilbert took everything thrown at him, and never went down. My father was proud of the fact that he went the distance, even though he was so spent that he couldn't lift his arms due to the weight of the heavy gloves. He would fight two more bouts with his shipmates before leaving boot camp and going on a two-week leave. It was late in the Spring of 1943, and having just turned eighteen, my dad already exhibited a toughness that he would benefit from, and need, in the months and years to follow.

While in basic training, Gilbert was given a series of aptitude tests to determine the job he was best suited for in the Navy. He, along with several other recruits, was chosen to report to Boston, Massachusetts, for communications schooling after his basic training was complete. He was ordered to report to the Somerset Hotel on Commonwealth Ave.

*"That was pretty good duty, living in a big hotel with good food and nice rooms... that is until we found out that we had to walk to and from school every day through the Boston Commons to Boylston and Washington Streets. Our school was at that intersection, on the top floor."* (4, 5)

During the Spring and Summer of 1943, my dad spent his days in both morning and afternoon classes, learning the basics of Navy communication: Morse code; ship-to-shore radio transmissions; and the use of various signal flags and hand-held devices. For lunch, he and his fellow classmates had to go down to street level to a place named the "Chicken Coop," which often served a mediocre fare of meat loaf, franks and beans, and spaghetti. While my father never complained about the quality of the food and usually ate what he was served, others in the school were not as happy.

*"It wasn't long before all of the guys staged a protest. We all got together and stayed in school one day, refusing to go downstairs for lunch. The lieutenant in charge was furious, and called it a mutiny. But it got results, for in the following weeks we were served better food."* (4, 6)

While my father studied during the day, in the evening he often availed himself of the boisterous Boston night life. Scollay Square was a magnet for the many servicemen and college students in the area who were tempted by the seamy side of what Boston had to offer. (8) My father related that one establishment, the Imperial House, was nothing but a bar for picking up prostitutes:

*"And one night a buddy of mine and I did just that. We bought them a few drinks and headed out to a movie theater down the street. We sat with them necking in the theater for about a half hour when I asked my friend if he needed to take a leak. He said yes, and we went to the rear of the theater, where we discussed our feelings for the hookers. He said he 'did not like the looks of his,' and I did not like the looks of mine either. So both of us bolted out the door into the night, and we never saw either of them again."* (4, 8)

There was also the infamous Old Howard, a theater that featured comedians, some of who were "pretty raw," and strippers, some of who were "very good and some very bad." (4, 8) My dad went to a few of these shows, maybe four or five times. He also went frequently to the Crawford House, which had shows that were much better than those at the Old Howard. My father's sister Lucille worked in the lounge at the

Crawford House and would slip him a few bucks every now and then, knowing full well that he wasn't making very much money in the Navy (recruits were paid twice a month, and the money was often spent within a week).

One night my dad went to the Crawford House alone, and his sister had him sit in a back-corner table where she gave him a few beers on the house. After a while she came back and asked him if would like to see the show in the main room. She then introduced Gilbert to the manager, who escorted him in. On stage there was a comedian and a few singers, along with a small band. After they performed their acts, out came the star of the show: a dancer named **Sally Keith**, the famous blonde "Tassel Tosser." Sally appeared on stage wearing a bikini top and bottom, with tassels hanging from each breast; one on the front of her bikini bottom; and one on her sequined derriere.

*"What she did with those things really amazed me. She would start with the front ones rotating in the same direction, then reverse them, then have them go in alternate directions. I couldn't for the life of me understand how she did that."* (4, 11)

After graduation from communications school in the Fall of 1943, the trainees were sent to different locations: some went directly aboard ships; some went on to further schooling; and some, like my dad, were sent to serve in the amphibious forces. Gilbert was assigned and reported to the newly formed 7th Naval Beach Battalion (NBB) at Camp Bradford in Little Creek, Virginia, just outside of Norfolk.

The 7th NBB was formally commissioned on October 5, 1943. It was initially formed by twelve transferees from Fort Pierce, Florida, and fourteen members of the previously established 3rd NBB. Additional men were then transferred in from the 1st, 2nd, 3rd, and 6th NBBs, as well as from the various communication schools and JASCO (Joint Assault Signal Company) units to round out the battalion. Officers were also transferred in from all departments of the Navy to provide leadership. (13) In this early formative stage, many in the battalion spent their time participating in "routine marching exercises and beach landings." (4, 7)

After the battalion's quota was finally filled, they were sent to Fort Pierce for more intensive practice landings.

NBBs were formed during World War II to assist Army units in amphibious landings in the African and European theater of operations, bridging the gap between sea and land. The units were independent of any specific ship and designed to handle all the necessary functions on an invasion beachhead. Even though they were in the Navy, NBBs were officially attached to the Army's Engineering Special Brigades (ESBs). NBBs were responsible for handling all ship-to-shore communications, clearing and marking sea lanes for landing craft and personnel, treating and evacuating casualties from the beach, and performing minor repairs on small boats. The operating commander of a NBB was the Beach Master, and he was in charge of everything (up to the high-tide line) on the sector of the beach he was assigned. Beach Masters have been called the "traffic cops of the invasion" because they directed the landing of every craft, regardless of its shape or size. (6, 227)

An NBB was composed of three companies: A, B, and C. Each company intern had three platoons, referenced by their company letter and a number in ascending sequence from one to nine (e.g., A-1, A-2, A-3, B-4, B-5, B-6, C-7, C-8, C-9). In order to meet its assigned duties, each NBB platoon had four sections: communications, hydrographic, medical, and small-boat repair. The communications section handled all Navy ship-to-shore messages, using blinker lights, signal flags, and radios. The hydrographic section was responsible for marking sea lanes, removing obstacles, and handling the ropes of the various landing craft. The medical section had a Doctor assigned to it to take care of casualties before evacuation, as well as Navy corpsmen who were responsible for getting casualties from the beach to the evacuation landing craft. The small-boat repair section repaired only minor breakdowns in their sector, but would later combine into one large unit to perform major repairs as needed. (6, 228)

An NBB platoon roster was composed of a Beach Master, an Assistant Beach Master, and a Doctor (all officers). The total number of enlisted men for each platoon was approximately forty three: the communication section had eight men (signalmen and radiomen); the hydrographic section contained roughly nineteen men; the medical section had eight men; and the boat-repair section had a quota of eight men. A complete NBB consisted of approximately 450 men. (13)

**Gilbert Dube (far left) training in the US prior to sailing for England**

The 7th NBB returned to Camp Bradford from Fort Pierce shortly before Christmas in 1943, and all of its members were given a short leave. They had endured months of rigorous training; training they knew was aimed at breaching Hitler's Atlantic Wall and Fortress Europe. They spent endless hours on obstacle courses and forced marches in loose beach sand while wearing field packs. They were often rousted out of their bunks at 0330 and ordered into small landing craft to rendezvous with cargo ships five miles off the coast. In fifteen-foot seas, they clambered up and down cargo nets with full packs. On many nights they slept in foxholes. (9)

Finally in early 1944, the men of the 7th NBB were transferred to a staging area at Lido Beach in Long Island, New York, prior to sailing for Great Britain aboard the **HMS Aquitania**.

The Aquitania docked in Gourock, Scotland, where most of the battalion boarded a train to southern England.

*"I believe we rode that train all night and a good part of the next day before we reached Plymouth."* (4, 8)

Upon arrival in Plymouth, they climbed on troop transports and drove through the narrow streets to Salcombe, Devon, England – their home base. Julius Shoulars noted that "while traveling to Salcombe, as we passed through the towns, the streets would be lined with people waving flags, and giving us the 'V' for Victory sign... we tossed the kids chewing gum and candy." (13)

For the next several days, members of the 7th NBB relaxed in Salcombe and waited for their orders. When they came, things changed quickly and drastically. From then on in the Spring of 1944, battalion members engaged in hectic and demanding training in preparation for the invasion of Europe.

*"The training we went through in the States was child's play compared to the routines we were going through now. The hikes weren't one or two hours like before; now they were half-days with full packs and rifles. We went over long hills and rough terrain until most of the men where completely drenched with perspiration. That was besides all of the [practice] beach landings in different parts of southern England, namely Plymouth, Exeter, Paignton, Torquay, and quite a few other towns that I can't recall."* (4, 9)

**7th NBB sailors, ready for invasion practice landings, England, May, 1944**

One practice landing that my father did recall in great detail occurred in the early morning hours of April 28, 1944, at Slapton Sands:

*"...because it was on such a huge scale compared to the other landings. I learned ...only long after the war that a few ships in our simulated invasion were sunk by German E-boats. I and a few other radiomen and corpsmen were cooking some C rations on the beach when we heard several explosions in the far distance with flames shooting in the air. None of us paid too much attention to that, thinking it was all part of the maneuvers. I learned later ...that it was not the case. It was for real."* (4, 10)

Exercise Tiger at **Slapton Sands** was a live-ammunition practice run for assault forces of the U.S. 4$^{th}$ Infantry Division, who were to land on D-Day at Utah Beach in Normandy. A large convoy that was maneuvering in Lyme Bay in the early hours of April 28 was attacked by nine German E-boats out of Cherbourg that had managed to evade Allied patrols. No warning of the presence of enemy boats had been received until LST (Landing Ship Tank) 507 was torpedoed at 0204. The ship burst into flames, and survivors abandoned ship. Several minutes later LST-531 was torpedoed and sank in six minutes. LST-289, which opened fire at E-boats, was also torpedoed but was able to reach port. The other LSTs involved, plus two British destroyers, fired at the E-boats, which used smoke and high speed to escape. This brief action resulted in 198 Navy dead and missing and 441 Army dead and missing, according to naval action reports. Later Army reports gave 551 as the total number of dead and missing soldiers. (5)

All was not work in England. Like he did in Boston, and like many Americans did while stuffed into the hundreds of encampments in southern England in the Spring of 1944, my father experienced the nightlife in the area – on the rare occasion when he could finagle a short liberty. At times though some of the servicemen didn't always get along with each other, especially when the attention of a young lady involved.

"*In Knightsbridge, a small town not too far from Salcombe, we used to go to a U.S.O. dance hall. We went to one of those dances on a Saturday night, and there were quite a few English girls and some American WACs there. Most of the English girls learned how to jitterbug quite well. I spotted one about my height and asked her to dance. She accepted, and onto the dance floor we went. I no sooner started to dance when a sailor tapped me on the shoulder, saying he was cutting in. I turned and told him that I had just got on the floor and kept on dancing, when he grabbed my arm and pulled at me, so I gave him a shove in the chest. That's when he said, 'OK buddy, let's go outside.' I couldn't back off, so outside we went. It was sort of comical; we started grabbing at each other, neither one wanting to throw a punch. We just kind of wrestled, throwing each other on the ground, when at one point I lifted him up by the leg ...and literally picked him up over my head and tossed him down an embankment that sloped down around four or five feet. Just then a couple of Shore Patrol intervened and broke up the fight. They gave us a lecture on how sailors on liberty should control themselves and act like gentlemen. They asked us to shake hands and go back inside, which we did. Needless to say, the sailor did not try to cut in again when I was back on the dance floor."* (4, 16)

Even though they were attached to the Army, the men of the NBBs were sailors first and foremost, and tried not to lose their Navy identity while surrounded by numerous Army troops. When on liberty, they wore their dress blue uniforms and bloused their baggy trousers into their boots. They took delight in telling the curious British civilians that they were "Navy Paratroops." The sailors in the 6th NBB even made a point to show up in their Navy blues, black scarves, and white hats when ordered by an Army commander to perform guard duty; an act that excluded them from ever having to perform such duty again. (6, 231)

Since the NBBs were in the position of being Navy sailors under Army control, their source of uniforms and supply was often confusing. Many of the NBBs in England had a mixture of Army and Navy issue gas masks; some battalions were issued paratrooper boots and some were not; some were issued Winter combat jackets, while others were given M41 field jackets. Each NBB section was also armed differently: the hydrographic section carried M1903 Springfield rifles; the small-boat repair and communication crews carried M1 carbines; the medical section was issued .45 pistols (primarily for guard duty in England); petty officers (NCOs) leading each section where given Thompson machine guns, and the platoon commander carried both an M1 carbine and a .45 pistol. (6, 231)

NBBs also sought to distinguish themselves from Army troops, and from other NBBs, through the use of **helmet markings**. Sailors in the 7th NBB placed an arc on the front of their helmets, followed below by the letters "USN" and the number "7," all painted in red. Other NBBs involved in the Normandy landings (the 2nd and 6th) had distinctively different markings. Shortly before the invasion, an order was given to all Navy troops who might operate on the beaches to paint a gray 2" band around their helmets, and the letters "USN" in large print on the front and back of their uniforms. The order served two purposes: it identified sailors who might be wearing unfamiliar uniforms to any trigger-happy Army soldiers; and it prevented sailors from being used for inland fighting by Army commanders while they still had work to do on the beach. (6, 232) Painting their helmets in this way as ordered also had the effect of partially obscuring the red "7" that was previously applied by members of the 7th NBB. (12)

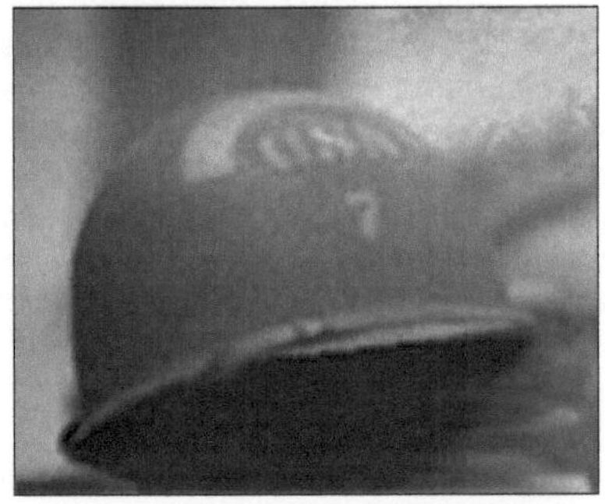

After months of intensive training along the beaches and coastline of southern England, my father, and the men of the 7th NBB, knew that the time for the real invasion was drawing near.

*"I think about four or five days before the invasion we were trucked to a bivouac area (to the west of Salcombe) that was all fenced in, and security was pretty strict. We couldn't get out of the area unless we were either too sick or dying."* (4, 11)

Those in battalions and companies identified to participate in the initial invasion were moved into position for final debarkation, and they were extensively briefed. They were told the objective was the western beaches of Normandy on the French coastline, and of the types of obstacles and their positions in the water with respect to the particular beach sectors. They were shown exact models and maps of enemy entrenchments. They were given the proposed locations for Army and Navy evacuation centers, ammunition dumps, water and supply depots and the areas to be taken by the Rangers and Airborne troops. They were also given several first aid demonstrations, gas mask drills, and lectures and demonstrations on German uniforms, markings, weapons, and equipment. (1, 2) At this time Naval Combat Demolition Units (NCDUs) were also formally placed under the administrative control of the NBBs, and were assigned to NBBs platoons in a special section to assist the hydrographic crew in obstacle clearance.

Just prior to the invasion, members of the 7th NBB were issued a two-piece, gas-impregnated suit. Also issued were lifebelts with $CO_2$ cartridges attached for instant inflation. Everyone had a special load to bring ashore. Signalmen like my father had to carry their radios (in heavy backpacks), blinker lights, and semaphore flags. Medics had to carry their litters, blankets, and extra field medical supplies. Platoon commanders carried an SCR-536 hand-talkie so that they could speak directly with Beach Masters on either side of them. (6, 234)

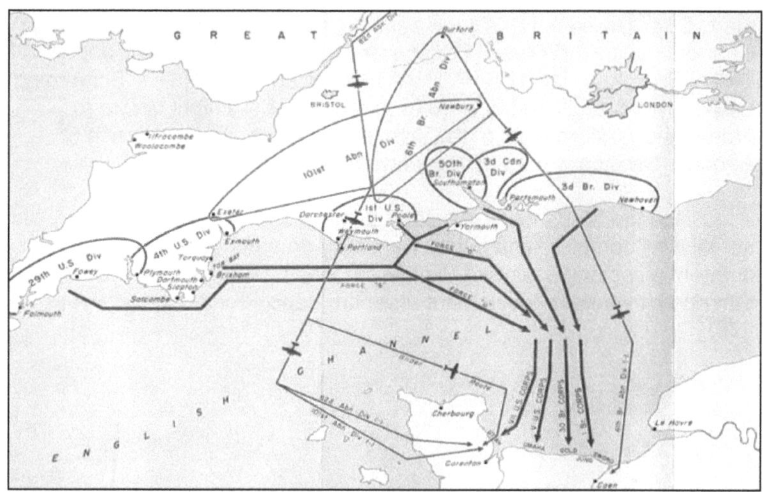


On June 4, 1944, members of the 7th NBB boarded various LST and LCI (Landing Craft Infantry) ships with full gear. *"Everybody knew that this was it."* (4, 11) Men waited below deck for further instructions. The rough weather in the English Channel caused a long delay, but the soldiers and sailors pressed on with their poker games, or whatever they did to occupy their time. Finally on the evening of June 5th, on board LST-372, the public address system came to life with the voice of General Eisenhower reading his "Great Crusade" speech. (10, 198)

June 6, 1944, would be D-Day for the Allied forces, the 7th NBB, and for Gilbert Dube. A Navy sailor – a nineteen-year old from Lewiston, Maine – would be storming the beach as a soldier. He would be stepping foot on French soil for the first time to help free the country from years of Nazi tyranny and oppression; the same country from which Mathurin Dubé emigrated in 1659 to establish the Dube family name in North America.

*"We sailed long after midnight until we could barely see sunrise and land in the distance. I don't believe many of us slept much that night."* (4, 11)

For the invasion, Companies B and C of the 7th NBB were attached to the Army's 6th ESB, which supported the U.S. 29th Infantry Division (the "Blue and Gray"). The 29th Division was to land in the western sectors of Omaha Beach (**Dog Green**, **Dog White**, **Dog Red**, and **Easy Green**). The 6th NBB was attached to the Army's 5th ESB, and it supported the U.S. 1st Division (the "Big Red One") which was to land in the eastern sectors of Omaha Beach (**Easy Red**, **Fox Green**, and **Fox Red**). On Utah Beach, to the west of Omaha Beach past Pointe Du

Hoc, the 2nd NBB was attached to the Army's 1st ESB, which supported the U.S. 4th Division. (7) To the east of Omaha Beach, British, Canadian and Free French forces were to land at Gold, Juno, and Sword Beaches. The U.S. 82nd ("All American") and 101st ( "Screaming Eagle") Airborne Divisions were to parachute in the night before to protect the western flank of the invasion beaches, and the British 6th Airborne Division was to do the same for the eastern flank.

Since the NBBs were considered important to the invasion, they did not land as complete units; they were split up among a number of different ships and assigned to different landing waves. This insured that one hit would not knock out an entire beach-control section. (6, 238)

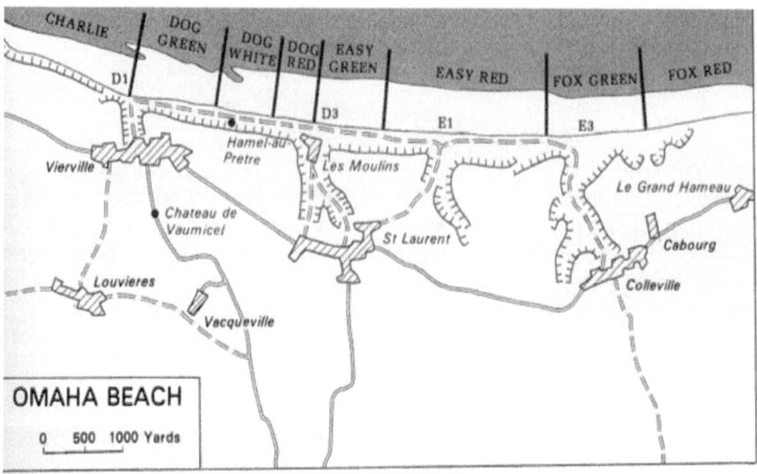


At daybreak on June 6, my father went topside on his LST and saw the greatest armada ever assembled in the history of warfare. For as far as his eyes could see, there were ships: cruisers, destroyers, tankers, freighters, transports, and hundreds of landing craft – LCIs, LSTs, and LCVPs (Landing Craft Vehicle Personnel). Some 2,000 ships in all. Gilbert knew that he would be getting on one of the LCVPs shortly for his journey to the Dog Red sector of Omaha Beach near the Les Moulins draw. He was worried but not scared, for he was told by command that the German defenses there consisted of nothing but "old men and children." (4, 12)

Each LST putting troops ashore at Omaha Beach had a specific plan for disembarking, and members of companies B and C of the 7th NBB were scattered across five separate waves of roughly 100 men each. Each wave would consist of twenty men from each of the 4 modified and enhanced sections of the battalion, plus the NCDUs. The first wave would leave at H-Hour, the second at H+1, the third at H+2, and so on. All participating members of the 7th NBB were scheduled to be ashore at Omaha Beach before Noon. (10, 198) At least that was the plan.

At 0600, while troops began clambering down cargo nets hanging from the sides of the LSTs into waiting LCVPs, the vast assemblage of warships opened up with a massive and coordinated forty-minute barrage at pre-selected targets, a barrage designed to soften the German defenses on the beach and provide cover for the incoming forces. Rockets from LSM(R)s and LCT(R)s were sending thousands of charges at the hilly terrain on the cliffs and behind the beach. (7) Now back below deck, my dad waited his turn to muster. He checked his equipment: a waterproof radio pack, life belt, M-1 carbine, gas mask, cartridge belt, and small field pack. All totaled it weighed more than half as much as he did.

*"I can't remember exactly when we were called to board the LCVPs. They announced the units in successive order, and things moved quickly. We then climbed to the main deck with our equipment, rifles, and packs and proceeded to drop down the rope cargo nets to our landing crafts. There were six or seven of them assembled. The sea was extremely choppy. When they were all loaded we moved away from the ship and started circling around for quite awhile, maybe a couple of hours or so. I noticed several of my shipmates were getting pretty sick and vomiting all over the place. I didn't throw up, but I still got a little woozy and quite pale."* (4, 13)

Beach Battalion sections were among some of the first waves to land on the shore. The landings, however, were not going as planned. A strong eastward current, and withering enemy fire, caused many of the troops to land in the wrong location. The first assault waves of the 29th and 1st Divisions were getting decimated on the beach due to heavier than expected opposition from the tough and experienced 352nd Infantry Division (which had moved into a defensive position above Omaha Beach only a few days before), and an opening barrage that turned out to be ineffective against the thick casements. (7) Many of the amphibious tanks in the first wave that were to support and give cover to the incoming troops were flooded and sunk immediately after they were launched. Those that made it to the beach were knocked out quickly. Out in the channel, pilot-less landing craft filled with dead GIs were circling aimlessly. Troop carriers LCI-91 and LCI-92 in the Dog White sector were beached and on fire. (2) The ESBs had such a hard time opening the exits from Omaha Beach that by 0830 a 7th NBB Beach Master (in the 29th Division sector) sent out an order to temporarily cease all landings of vehicles on the beach – there was simply no more room and no way to get the vehicles off of it. (6, 236)

On board his circling LCVP, Gilbert heard the coxswain say it was finally time to head in to the beach. It was now around 1000 in the morning.

*"That's when I began to freeze up a bit. I was paralyzed. I remember praying and hoping that this wasn't my last day on earth… that I would live out the day."* (4, 13)

The ramp went down, and my dad hit the water – a water tinged red from the blood of those who landed before him. He was soon wading in the surf up to his chest and sometimes going under – partly because he was a short man, partly because he was stepping into some shell holes, and partly because he was carrying a large amount of equipment, now completely soaked. All around him, he heard deep "thumps" in the water and on the beach as the German 88 mm guns and various mortars were pummeling his sector with sustained, accurate fire.

Despite this, my father felt quite relieved because he was finally off of the pitching LCVP, and it appeared, for now, that the beach directly in front of him was not very "hot." Timing, or so it seems, was everything. Gilbert then scurried across 100 yards or so of open ground.

*"When we finally got closer to the beach …I didn't hear rifle or machine gun fire that was close enough to hit us. But there was a lot of it coming from over the bluff, along with the 88s."* (4, 14)

**The shingle, and remnants of the sea wall and bunkers on Omaha Beach**

My father wasted no time in crawling to a three-foot high sea wall near a bank of small round stones (called "shingle") that sloped towards the beach, a wall that offered cover from sniper fire and incoming artillery barrages. He dug in among the stones, where he remained for a good part of the morning and afternoon. While hunkered down, my dad was able to survey the scene around him. It was pure carnage. Dead soldiers lay the way they last fought. Some were in grotesque positions, with arms extended and open mouths frozen in the voice of pain. (11, 8)

While the fighting in the Dog Red sector at that point was not as intense as it was in the adjacent sectors (Dog Green, Dog White, and Easy Green), the situation was desperate nonetheless. Lieutenant Carpenter, the assigned Beach Master on Dog Red, requested that the communications section send a message to the flagship asking for supplies and additional men on the beaches. Garwood Bacon, a Yeoman in the 7th NBB, worked with a radioman on the beach for about an hour before the message got through. Later, Bacon ventured down the beach some two hundred yards (as Dog Red was not his assigned sector), crouching along the sea wall for cover while looking for his commanding officer. He soon found himself in the midst of about fifty to seventy-five men, all lying prostrate in the sand. Thinking that they were lying there because they were pinned down by gunfire, he threw himself down between two soldiers and buried his face in the sand. After no gunfire was heard, he lifted his head to see that one of the men he had dropped between was headless, and the other was blown half apart. Every last one of them was dead, killed by machine gun fire and 88s during the assault wave. (10, 192)

It was not until 1340 that the beaches in the Dog and Easy sectors were clear of opposition, except for artillery and mortar fire. Slowly the fighting moved inland, but the beaches continued to be subject to enemy shelling which, while neither heavy or sustained, was dead-on accurate. The artillery barrages by the Germans were obviously observed, because enemy batteries would remain silent until craft were beached ...and then there would be a few quick salvos, usually right on target. This artillery fire caused considerable loss and was especially frustrating because neither enemy observers or artillery batteries could be quickly located. In fact, repeated requests for U.S. vessels to cease firing on the beaches were made by personnel ashore, as well as seaward observers, who thought that U.S. ships were firing into their own troops. In actuality, no U.S. ships were firing at the time the requests were made, and when they did fire, they were firing at targets inland, rather than on the beach. (7)

Later on in the day when the situation on Omaha Beach was somewhat stabilized and there was a lull in the battle, my father started roaming up and down the various sectors to assess the damage. Only then did he realize the supreme effort and ultimate sacrifice made by the men of the 29th Division, the 1st Division, the 5th and 6th ESBs, and the 6th and 7th NBBs.

*"There were quite a few bodies and parts of bodies scattered all over, some recognizable and some not. What struck me the most was the position they were in when they got hit and died, not only on the beach, but near the sea wall and beyond as well. Many bodies were on the slopes heading up to the top of the bluffs. One soldier was there still clutching his rifle, with clouded glasses on his face. I remember that I couldn't see his eyes. Dead soldiers were stacked up like cordwood. Those were scenes that stuck with me for many years."* (4, 15)

One scene that was particularly disturbing and haunted my dad's dreams long after the war dealt with a face he found floating in the water, along with other tragic flotsam from the battle:

*"Late in the afternoon I was walking around on the beach near the edge of the water. I kept looking around noticing all the scattered articles and debris in the sand and surf, like dented helmets, broken rifles, backpacks, etc. I happened to go near one of the LCVPs that was charred and still smoldering. On one side of the craft I saw something floating back and forth in the surf. It would come in off the water, and then another wave would wash it back out to sea. It was the side of a man's face, with part of his hair, eye, nose and mouth still visible and intact. I stood there and kept looking at it for quite a while. I then moved down the beach, but I came back to that spot and stared at the face again. I must have done this two or three times; I just couldn't get over it. I kept looking for the rest of the body, but it wasn't there. I kept thinking about that guy and kept asking myself 'Where is the rest of him?'"* (4, 24)(11, 8)

He also discovered later that day that one of his 7$^{th}$ NBB buddies, John R. Carhuff from New York City, was killed by enemy fire earlier in the morning. Carhuff, who was married and the father of two small children, was a corpsman (PhM2c) in the medical section of my dad's platoon. My father then went over to John's lifeless body on the beach to pay his final respects.

While the 6$^{th}$ and 7$^{th}$ NBB suffered many casualties during the landings, the attached NCDUs were hit especially hard, due to the nature of their duties (beach obstacle removal and demolition) and the fact that they were often included in the first assault waves in all of the supported sectors. NCDU losses were:

| Dead | 24 | (4 officers and 20 enlisted) |
|---|---|---|
| Wounded | 32 | (3 officers and 29 enlisted) |
| Missing | 15 | (0 officers and 15 enlisted) |
| Total | 71 | (7 officers and 64 enlisted) |

This equated to 41% of their total strength. (7)

**The Dog Red Sector on Omaha Beach – June 8, 1944**

As night fell on the Dog Red sector, the American forces tenuously held onto their foothold on Omaha Beach. Hitler's Atlantic Wall had been breached, and some of the units had started to move deep inland. Allied forces had made excellent gains on Utah, Gold, Juno, and Sword Beaches. The western and eastern flanks of the invasion beaches had been secured. But along Omaha, the front barely stretched for a mile inland, and less than that in some sectors. The beach was still in a state of confusion and cluttered with troops, vehicles, and landing craft – so much so that some members of the 7th NBB who were scheduled to land on D-Day were delayed until D+1 by the Beach Masters. (13) Rumors of a pending German counter attack that would cut the invasion front in two, and push the American forces back into the sea, ran rampant among the various units on the beach. (4, 16)

The shelling continued, but despite this, the NBBs continued on with their work: clearing sea lanes for incoming craft; setting up ship-to-shore communications nets; and aiding casualties on the beach. The medical sections started moving the wounded to casualty collection points, wounded who would eventually be evacuated to landing craft that would shuttle them out to a hospital ship, and back to England.

The first night on the beach was the most memorable for my father. Before dark, he was told to dig a foxhole beyond the sea wall, ten to twenty yards in the flat before the edge of the bluff behind him. My dad dug his foxhole fairly deep because he wanted to stand up to see all around his position. He placed dirt on both sides of the foxhole, and near the top of his head he laid his gas mask and rifle. As he settled in for the night, he heard a lot of moaning and crying for help, mainly for medics. In the early morning hours, when it was nearly pitch black on the beach, my dad had an unwelcome visitor:

*"As I was looking towards the ocean, what appeared to my right was the figure of a man kneeling on one knee. It didn't bother me too much at first until he started moving directly towards me. He moved quietly and deliberately. He knelt down again looking in all directions – to his right, and left, and towards the ocean. That's when I noticed his cap. He had on one of those long-peaked caps like a lot of the Germans wore. My carbine was just out of reach, and I froze and didn't move a muscle for what felt like an eternity. I thought he was going to jump in and stab me. My heart was pounding so hard I thought for sure he would hear it. He then got up and started moving again to my left, towards Pointe Du Hoc. I lifted my head ever so slowly and watched him move further down the beach. It was the scariest moment of my life. "* (4, 17)

The next morning, after a breakfast of K rations, my father asked some of the sailors in the foxholes around him if any of them had seen the man with the peaked cap. None of them had.

On D+1, and for the days following, the communication sections of the NBBs continued with their ship-to-shore transmissions. Watches were setup, and visual contact was made with approaching landing craft using blinker lights and semaphore flags. Massive amounts of men and equipment were pouring onto the beachhead at a furious pace as the troops continued to push inland and establish a foothold in Normandy. Many of the men worked around the clock for the first few days without any sleep at all. As ships approached, it was determined which beach was their destination, which units or cargoes they were carrying, and whether or not they wished to unload. (10, 200) At the same time, the Germans were still lobbing artillery onto the beach, sending shrapnel along the sand and water. The casualties continued to mount.

*"...this guy named Hornburger, who was also a radioman like me, was hit by shrapnel in the upper arm. He wasn't more than 2 or 3 yards away from me. Nearly every night right after dark we would get ready for the 88s to start shelling beach, trying to sink or destroy landing craft and disrupt the troops. This went on for three or four nights before it finally stopped."* (4, 19)

Conditions on Omaha Beach remained chaotic. There was no water available for bathing or shaving. There was only a limited amount of fresh water for drinking, and limited K rations to eat. The dead remained where they were, as the removal and graves registration teams had not yet had time to do their work. Sometimes, the equipment coming ashore had to run over some of the bodies. (10, 217) Unforeseen problems arose due to the huge numbers of men and materials being brought to shore. Troops were ditching their life belts and gas masks as soon as they hit the beach; by D+3 thousands of them had littered the area, making rapid passage impossible. A solution was found when NBB members acquired some fifty-foot rolls of meshed fence from the Army engineers and fashioned large circular bins. When not actively engaged in their duties, many of the sailors spent their time picking up the life belts and gas masks and pitched them into the bins, making walking along the beach much easier. (10, 231)

Minefields on and along the beach also continued to pose problems. The Germans had planted mines everywhere – in the sand, on the roads, and in the fields and hillsides throughout Normandy. The Army, using detectors, had cleared paths for the new arrivals to use to reach their destinations. The pathways were clearly marked and separated from the dangerous areas using strips of white tape. Additionally, signs that read "Keep Out Mines" and "Achtung Meinen" were posted throughout these areas. Nonetheless, either through stupidity or illiteracy, soldiers would sometimes dash under the tape to retrieve a German helmet or some other war souvenir. As a result, some of the men lost their legs, and some of the men lost their lives. (10, 232)

My dad wasn't exempt from such souvenir hunting, except in his first case it was driven more out of practical comfort than material gain. One day he saw a dead German soldier in one of the trenches along the bluffs who had roughly his shoe size, and he decided to liberate him of his black boots. My father didn't wear them for long however, out of fear of being mistaken for a German masquerading as a U.S. soldier. He quickly tossed them away. (4, 20)

On D+6, my dad noted that conditions on Omaha Beach began to improve. Small tents and bed rolls were issued to the troops. The sailors were also given fresh water for drinking and bathing. Soon after that, the engineers put up a huge tent, complete with a kitchen and large stove, along with benches and seats. "All the comforts of home." Food, however, remained a major source of contention for the soldiers. Although K rations became plentiful, they were generally awful. They contained small cans of cheese or ham and eggs, biscuits that tasted like dog food, a compressed bar of raisins, figs, and prunes, sometimes a bitter-chocolate bar, and small packets of instant coffee, tea, or chocolate. This grew old in a hurry, and the men became restless. (10, 203) When men become restless, they also become resourceful.

The sailors started scavenging for better food sources, and soon discovered Army C rations. These cans were the size used for canned soup, and they contained delicacies like corned beef and hash, beef stew, and franks and beans. When heated in mess kits, they were a big improvement over K rations. Often a cartoon of C rations would fall off a truck. Other times the NBB members would mooch a carton from a soldier riding on top of a supply truck. More than once, sailors hopped aboard slow-moving convoys and liberated a carton or two. (10, 203) My father and his partners went so far as to raid the kitchens on the LSTs that were ashore, looking for food and supplies. Some of it they would hoard in their tents, and some of it they would use later on in the French villages for bartering and humanitarian purposes.

By June 12th, the Beach Masters of the 2nd, 6th, and 7th NBBs on Utah and Omaha beaches had facilitated the movement of up to 9,452 tons of material per day. On June 15 the Navy Seabees completed a Mulberry Harbor, and the first vehicles rolled off an LST directly onto the floating piers and dry land. Unloading cargo was no longer dependent on the tides, and things were flowing smoothly – that is until a storm on June 19 hit the Normandy coastline. Many small craft and vessels were beached by the storm and damaged beyond repair. The Mulberry Harbor was completely ruined. A serious supply and ammunition shortage ensued. The storm had left the beaches in worse shape than they were after the initial landings. The Beach Battalions, along with other units stationed on the shore, cleared the debris in record time and got many of the small craft repaired and back into operation. (10, 241)

As a steady stream of German prisoners of war (POWs) began to make their way to the beach before being transported to England, and eventually to the U.S., some members of the NBBs were called upon to act as guards. William DeFrates, a signalman in the 7th NBB, had one such experience along with three other sailors.

*"On D+17 ...200 German prisoners pulled up to our station and stopped. This is how four Navy signalmen with M-1 carbines came to stand guard ...until 0700 the following morning. The captured men were as meek as lambs. Nothing equals the blank stare in the eyes of a defeated soldier. They neither knew nor cared what befell them. One of them showed us his field rations. It looked like ...sawdust."* (10, 203)

**A member of the 2nd NBB leads German POWs along Utah Beach**

As Omaha Beach became totally secured, and the front had advanced inland for miles, many of the sailors in the NBBs, including my father, started venturing off the beach and into the towns of the Norman countryside, looking for whatever they could find.

*"Me and my buddies would visit towns and villages, namely St. Laurent, Carentan, and St. Mere Eglise not long after they were liberated. Most of them were deserted, and inside the homes there was debris scattered all over. We were mostly looking for souvenirs, or anything of value we could find, mainly booze and money. But given the way those houses were in such disarray, we knew that we weren't the first ones there and just about gave up on finding anything of value. One sailor though found a pile of French Francs, and ditched his gas mask to use the bag to hold his loot. I heard he would turn some of them into the paymaster once a week to send money orders home. He told them that he had won it gambling at cards and craps, which was believable since there was a lot of that stuff going on. One day in St. Laurent I spotted a car radio in a small house, and latched onto that in a hurry. It was one of the best things I found, because we were able to listen to the BBC for news, and good music as well. I had it hooked up to a regular truck battery and when the signal became weak, I would take it back to the motor pool and exchange it for another, or wait and have it charged."* (4, 23)

Gilbert also frequently visited the town of Vierville-sur-Mer, just above the bluffs of Omaha Beach in the highly contested Dog Green sector. There he befriended a family named Dumont. Even though he spoke his French with a French-Canadian dialect, my father was able to easily communicate with them. He remembers his first encounter with the beleaguered family:

*"They were eating dinner and all they had was a loaf of dark bread. I could see that they didn't have much to eat. They were elated when we later brought them some food."* (11, 8)

He gave the family cigarettes to smoke and food to eat. He started by giving them K rations, but later he and his buddies raided the company larder and gave them canned beef stew and peaches. My father's charity to the family in the presence of a great catastrophe was highly appreciated; the grateful locals reciprocated with the local apple brandy (Calvados), cognac, and homemade beer.

By the end of June, the port of Cherbourg had fallen, and since beach landings we no longer required at Omaha or Utah, most members of the 2nd, 6th, and 7th NBBs returned to England for reassignment. The first group to leave went back to Salcombe, England, to prepare for a second invasion in the south of France. When that invasion did not materialize, the men were shipped back to the U.S, to Lido Beach, Long Island, to await further orders. The 7th Naval Beach Battalion was then officially decommissioned by the Navy, with most of its former members receiving travel orders to Oceanside, California, for duty in the Pacific theater of operations. (13)

My father, because of his ability to speak French and act as a translator with the locals, volunteered to stay on in Normandy until the middle of August. Other members of the communication section volunteered to stay as well. During this time, they sought to break the monotony of what had become their daily routine. After all, they were now sailors in port.

*"Except for roll call or muster in the mornings, we were pretty much free to do anything we wanted to. We didn't have any specific duties except for rifle and short arms inspections every now and then. After Cherbourg was liberated, I headed there right away because I knew it was a large city. Me and my buddy Vinny, a short Italian guy who was always grinning, went around looking for pubs and cafes. We found one on a small side street and went in for a few cognacs. There were three or four Frenchmen inside and I started to speak French with them. They had no problem understanding me. So I eventually asked them where the local house of 'ill repute' was located. They replied that there was one just around the corner. Vinny and I then finished our drinks and headed for the house. This was our first time in Cherbourg, and this time there were no MPs in front of the hostel. The next time we went, they were there. But that didn't stop us; we exchanged our clothes for some French attire and went right in."* (4, 27)

My father's escapades continued, sometimes for longer than he had planned, and often with unexpected results:

*"I was doing my usual strolling around the different villages, hitching rides here and there, when one day a soldier picked me up in his jeep and we traveled all day, stopping occasionally for a sip of wine or cognac anyplace they were available. Pretty soon we realized we were quite a ways from the beachhead. We wound up in Rennes, and by then it was almost nightfall. We went into a little café to have another drink and decided it was too late to head back. We started asking around for a place to sleep. The town was in disarray, and we could hear the sound of artillery, tanks, and cannons blasting away, giving us warning that the front was not too far off. We found a little café and boarding house, and the proprietor was delighted when he learned that I could speak French. He took us upstairs and ushered us into a room with two large beds, and told us to make ourselves at home. It took awhile for me to fall asleep, since the building was rumbling and shaking from the artillery, but I finally nodded off. In the morning the owner had coffee and dark bread ready for us. I asked him how much we owed for the bed and breakfast, and to my surprise he said 'nothing, it was a*

*pleasure to have you in my home.' We then emptied our pockets of the goodies we had left and gave them to him. The soldier had a carton of cigarettes in the jeep, and he took a few packs out and brought them into the house.*

*And so on we went, heading back to the beach, stopping now and then in some small towns and villages along the way. In one town we went into this house that was deserted and ransacked. As we came out we noticed a shed to the rear, so we went back for a look. The door was padlocked, so I went around the side to a window, which I managed to pry open. We both went in and saw that it was a storage shed for old furniture and the like. We were about to climb back out of the window when I noticed some …large bottles with wicker around them. I grabbed one and uncorked it. It smelled like cognac, so I took a swig. Sure enough it was the real thing. There were several bottles there, but we only took one, which was more than enough for us. We climbed out the window with the bottle and back into the jeep when I heard someone shouting (in French) down the road 'Thieves!' We got the hell out of there, and when I looked back I could see them waving their arms in the air, and they were still shouting at us.*

*We stopped at another small town and filled our canteens with the cognac. A couple of soldiers observed us doing this and strolled over with their canteens in hand. Naturally we filled theirs, and then two Frenchmen came along with some jars, and we filled theirs too. I had that big jug on the edge of the jeep when it slipped out of my hands and crashed on the cobblestones, flowing its contents into the street. The two Frenchmen then got on their hands and knees and, licking their fingers, tried to save the last drops from the jug.*

*We hit the road, sipping from our canteens every now and then as we went along. By the time we reached the beachhead we were pretty well smashed. It was around Noon, and the soldier let me off by a big food tent where I grabbed something to eat. I then proceeded to join my company, and everyone was glad to see me but was worried because I wasn't there for roll call earlier in the morning. It was then that the lieutenant made an appearance and started to reprimand me. He gave me a pretty good scare, telling me that he was ready to list me as MIA. He also told me in so many words that if I pulled this type of stuff again, he would court martial me. I respected him for not taking any privileges away, and not even restricting me to the beach area. I was a pretty good little boy after that episode."* (4, 37)

On August 19, 1944, the remaining members of what was the 7$^{th}$ NBB turned over their duties to the 6$^{th}$ ESB, and were ordered to board an LST back to Salcombe, England. My father's stay on the beaches of Normandy was over. He made one last raid of the kitchen supplies and brought them to the Dumont family in Vierville-sur-Mer. He bid farewell, hoping one day that he would see them again after the war. As fate would have it, that did not happen.

Gilbert wasn't in England for long when he received word that he would be going aboard the **Queen Mary**, known at the time as the "Gray Ghost" (due to the World War II paint job) for his return trip to the U.S. My dad didn't realize just how big a ship the Queen Mary was until he was aboard. The ship was loaded with military personnel, as well as many wounded soldiers and sailors. There were also German POWs on board who were separated from the rest of the passengers by wire barriers and padlocked gates.

*"I tried to communicate with some of them, trying to tell them that Berlin was now 'kaput.' They kept waving back at me, saying 'nein, nein.'"* (4, 39)

The voyage home took about seven days, and along the way my father enjoyed good food and great entertainment from some of the musicians and performers aboard who donated their time and talent. However, he was a little disappointed that Sally Keith was not among them.

With the coast of the U.S. in view, everyone went topside, anxious to reach port.

*"When we started to see the New York City skyline, you should have heard the whooping and cheering from everyone. We then went by the Statue of Liberty. I had the most wonderful feeling in the pit of my stomach, a feeling I'm sure everyone else on board had as well. It was a feeling of pride that I cannot fully explain. "* (4, 40)

Back at Lido Beach, Long Island, my father, like the former members of the 7$^{th}$ NBB who arrived before him, was given orders to report to Camp Pendleton in Oceanside, California. After a long leave, he took a train to his new assignment. During the Spring of 1945, while still a member of the amphibious forces, Gilbert began to train for maneuvers and beach landings alongside Marine Corps personnel. He assumed at the time that he would soon be called upon to assist in the various beach landings on the Japanese occupied islands of the Pacific.

While the routine was all too familiar to him, his time off was far from normal; it was some of the best liberty he enjoyed while in the Navy.

*"We had every other night and weekend off. We headed for Los Angeles and Hollywood among a lot of other fabulous places like Long Beach, Santa Monica, Beverly Hills, San Pedro, and Balboa Beach. Of all these places, the most enjoyable was Hollywood. At the* ***Hollywood Canteen****, I mixed and mingled with a lot of famous movies stars of that time, such as Bette Davis, George Raft, James Cagney, and many others. The next best place was the Hollywood Palladium where I saw a lot of big bands and singers.*

*On one Saturday afternoon a buddy and I went out pub crawling. We wound up in this bar where I recognized an actor by the name of Wallace Ford, who was sitting with another actor (I can't recall his name) at a table nearby. He noticed that I kept looking at him, so he motioned for us to come over to his table and join him. We did, and he immediately ordered a round of drinks and asked me if I knew his name, which of course I did. His face lit up with a big smile. My friend and I put a few bills on the table for the next round, which he picked up and stuffed back into our breast pockets. We spent the whole afternoon there telling stories and jokes with each other. No need to tell you that none of us walked out of that bar sober."* (4, 43)

The good times in California soon came to an end. My dad received new orders – this time to board a troop transport for Hawaii. When he arrived on the island of Oahu towards the middle of June, 1945, he was assigned to bivouac in a large tent, which held ten to twelve sailors each. He remained there for three weeks until finally all the various amphibious units were broken up and the men reassigned for duty on different ships. Gilbert was assigned to the USS Scania AKA-40, an Artemis-class attack cargo ship. For the first time since enlisting in the Navy on December 28, 1942, my father would now be serving a tour of duty at sea.

On July 15, 1945, the Scania departed Pearl Harbor, Hawaii, carrying cargo for the islands of Tarawa, Majuro, and Kwajalein. After her return to Pearl Harbor on August 8, she made local cargo voyages in the Hawaiian Islands until sailing on September 7 for Canton Island, Espiritu Santo, Eniwetok, and Wake. On arrival at Wake Island on

October 11, the Scania reported for "Magic Carpet" duties. The ship made two voyages carrying troops home, one from Eniwetok and one from Tacloban in the Philippines before being released from Magic Carpet duty in Los Angeles at the end of December. On January 17, 1946, the Scania sailed from San Pedro, California, and began a year of duty carrying cargo in the western Pacific. She made four voyages from Guam during this period, calling at Manus, the Philippines, Okinawa, Japan, and China. (3)

My dad found his experiences on board the Scania to be quite different, and dull, from those in the 7$^{th}$ NBB. When at sea, he worked in the radio room for four hours on and eight hours off.

*"All we did was sit there with these headphones on and watched typewriters receive coded messages in five-letter groupings. It was sort of boring and monotonous. We would go from one island to another delivering and receiving all kinds of supplies and personnel. Most of the islands looked about the same to me, sort of barren and desolate. There were other ports we went to that were a little better, like in the Philippines and Shanghai.*

*In Shanghai, I never saw such a murky and dirty river in my life. There were a lot of those small boats with bamboo partitions that people lived in, cooked on, and slept in all along the river. You could smell the foul odor of fish and other foods cooking. The streets in the city weren't any better ...but then again there were other places of interest in different parts of the city."* (4, 46)

Finally, while island hopping in the Pacific, my father earned enough points to separate from the Navy and return home. He got word to pack his gear and board a troop transport headed to the U.S. My dad was at sea for quite a few days before he reached the Panama Canal. From there he sailed up the Atlantic to the familiar coast of Norfolk, Virginia. He was then issued travel orders for the trip to Boston, and told to report to the Fargo Building to receive his separation papers and back pay.

*"It wasn't long after I hit the street that I hailed a cab for North Station for the train ride back to Lewiston. Before I took the train, I had a little shopping spree. I got myself a new shirt, tie, sport coat, slacks, and a pair of shoes. I went into the men's room and shed my Navy blues. I put on my new outfit, looked at myself in the mirror, and shouted at the top of my lungs "I am now a happy civilian!"* (4, 49)

Gilbert H. Dube was discharged from the U.S. Navy on May 30, 1946. He had just turned twenty-one years old. His World War II service took him across the U.S. from Boston to Los Angeles and Hawaii; to the shores of England and France; to the many islands of the Pacific; the Philippines; and finally to Shanghai, China.

After the war, my dad returned to Lewiston, went to work there in the local mills, and married my mother, the former Georgette Lafrance, on July 3, 1948. They had three children and lived a comfortable middle-class existence in New Jersey and Maine until 1987, when they retired and moved to Palm Bay, Florida, to live out their golden years.

In 1998, Gilbert and Georgette Dube celebrated their fiftieth wedding anniversary at a surprise party given by his children. Also in 1998, my dad and I both saw the film *Saving Private Ryan*. I knew my father had participated in the D-Day landings, but I didn't know many of the details. He didn't like to talk about it all that much. But after seeing the film, which affected me greatly and sparked my interest in the event, I pressed him for information, and he finally opened up.

He told me that even though he was a sailor in the Navy, he landed on the beach, on Omaha Beach, and functioned just like a soldier. He told me of the horrors he saw, the fears he had, and the escapades he engaged in while in France. He also told me that *Saving Private Ryan* was incredibly accurate in its depiction of the D-Day landings, and that he too was deeply moved by the film. He even noted that members of the 7$^{th}$ NBB were shown in several of the opening scenes. I then asked if he had ever been back to Normandy, and he replied "no."

For Christmas that year, I gave him and my mom an all-expense-paid " Return To Normandy" tour as a present. I also gave him two blank notebooks, and asked him to start writing his memoirs of the war.

In June of 1999, my dad returned to Normandy for the fifty-fifth commemoration of the D-Day landings. We joined up with a military tour company in London, England, and then crossed the English Channel to the Normandy coast – just like my father did some fifty-five years earlier. In peace we toured the battlegrounds that my dad had known only in war. To him, some things were very different, and in some ways they were the same as he remembered. Now there were so many memorials to see, so many cemeteries to visit, and so many ceremonies to attend.

One of the highlights of the trip was when we stopped at Omaha Beach, near the town of Vierville-sur-Mer, to visit a memorial to the 29$^{th}$ Infantry Division that was built atop an old German bunker nearby. As I took photographs, my father then took his first steps back onto Omaha Beach (near the Dog Green sector) since August of 1944. Shortly thereafter, a fellow tourist, who was British, made a point to pin a "D-Day Veteran" medal onto my dad's chest. It was a moment of kindness and honor I will never forget. Unfortunately, our visit at Omaha was all too brief. On our way back to the tour bus, my father asked some locals in the area if they had ever heard of a family named Dumont. They said they did not, and so we had to move on.

**Father and son on Omaha Beach – June 7, 1999**

Back aboard the bus, the tour guide asked my dad to sit up front and say a few words to the group about his experiences on Omaha Beach. My father started to speak, but he could not finish.

The next stop on our itinerary was the American Cemetery at Colleville-sur-Mer, which lies just above the eastern part of Omaha Beach, near what was the Fox Green sector. I remembered my dad saying that one of his buddies was killed on D-Day, so I stopped at the cemetery's information desk to see if he was buried there by chance. He was. **John R. Carhuff** rests in peace in Plot I, Row 14, Grave 21.

Our English counterparts on the tour were especially gracious hosts, and they treated my father with great respect and admiration, particularly after they were informed that he had landed on Omaha Beach on the morning of June 6, 1944. They bought him drinks, hung on his every word, laughed at his corny jokes, and thoroughly enjoyed the company of the short, stocky American. My dad and I made many friends during the trip, and continued to keep in touch and visit with some of them long after the tour was completed.

Years later he confided to me that it was one of the most rewarding vacations of his life.

**My father and his British friends on the tour bus**

After an operation to remove a cancerous tumor from his lung, Gilbert H. Dube passed away on the morning of February 22, 2003, with his family by his side. He was seventy-seven years old.

Gilbert's wife Georgette, also after a long and courageous battle with cancer, joined him in heaven on October 12, 2003. She was seventy five.

The Provisional Government of France awarded the Croix de Guerre with Palm, the country's highest honor, to the 7th Naval Beach Battalion for its service on Omaha Beach. (12) Companies B and C of the 7th NBB were also awarded an Army Presidential Unit Citation, having been attached to the Army's 6th Engineering Special Brigade for the D-Day landings. (16) Due to a paperwork snafu between the Army and Navy bureaucracies during and long after World War II, members of the 6th Naval Beach Battalion, which was attached to the Army's 5th Engineering Special Brigade, had to wait for fifty-six years for their Army Presidential Unit Citation to be awarded. This injustice was finally corrected in June of 2000. (15)

The shore-based sailors of the NBBs have slowly started to receive the recognition they so rightly deserve. Films such as *Saving Private Ryan*, noting the involvement of the 7th NBB on D-Day, have helped to raise the public's awareness. Military author Jonathan Gawne notes that "the NBBs played not only a critical role in the initial landings in Normandy, but also in continuing to keep a steady flow of men and material moving swiftly across the beaches." However, he continued, "the U.S. Navy, for the most part, has all but forgotten them." (6, 226)

The U.S. Naval Historical Center contains no "official reports" of Naval Beach Battalion participation in the invasion. Archival files only verify that during the war, these specialized Navy units underwent intensive amphibious training at Camp Bradford in Little Creek, Virginia. Why the Navy has until now ignored the contributions of the Naval Beach Battalions in France and elsewhere remains unclear. Some have suggested a continuation of Navy secrecy regarding amphibious warfare during World War II. Others speculate that the NBBs were associated too closely with the Army's 1st, 5th, and 6th Engineering Special Brigades. (2)

The letter that follows, sent to the 7th NBB members prior to a recent reunion, shows that things are starting to change for the better. Personally, I think it's about damn time this happened.

# Chief of Naval Operations

TO THE MEMBERS OF
7TH BEACH BATTALION

Please accept my best wishes as you gather for your reunion. Those who served in our Beach Battalions in World War II deserve our sincere appreciation for their devoted service and personal sacrifice.

The example of courage and fortitude you set during the invasion of Normandy inspires our young service men and women to this day. Certainly what Americans see in our impressive Sailors and Marines -- in the men and women of all our armed services -- is the tradition of victory and dedication you established with your blood, your sacrifices and your valor.

Gatherings such as yours are important not only for members of your organization but for our country as well. We must not let our memory of dead and missing shipmates be dulled by the passage of time. We cannot afford to forget that our military forces must always be ready to defend our freedom and our national interests.

On behalf of the men and women of the U.S. Navy, please accept my best wishes for a rewarding and enjoyable reunion.

J.M. Boorda

J. M. BOORDA
Admiral, United States Navy
Chief of Naval Operations

## Epilogue

As I stood over my father's grave for the first time at the Florida National Cemetery in Bushnell, I was filled with ambivalent emotions. My dad had lived a full life, raised a family, was affable to and well liked by his friends and relatives, and retired after years of hard work. But he was by no means a perfect man, a perfect husband, or a perfect father. He was proud and stubborn. He struggled with bouts of alcoholism during his life. At times he disappointed his wife and his children with his actions. In his last few years, as his health and body failed him, he was a different person altogether, often mean and vindictive.

Yet, as I grew older and learned more about his service during D-Day and World War II, I accepted my father for who he was. He grew up during the Great Depression, and not having much material wealth, decided to live life to the fullest anyway. As a member of the Greatest Generation, he answered the call of duty and did what was expected of him. He didn't consider himself a hero, and didn't talk much about the war until I prompted him to do so. The war forced him to see and experience horrors that no nineteen-year old should ever have to endure. He participated in one of the most important and pivotal events in modern-day history, and after that he, like many other veterans of his time, went on to quietly pursue the American dream.

My dad knew that I was aware of this; that I respected and admired what he did for his country, and this helped to bridge the distance between us – the inevitable generation gap that developed when I was growing up as a teenager in the Dube household. As I matured, I began sharing an interest in the big-band music of his era, a result of hearing endless hours of it when I was a child. We talked often about boxing, his favorite sport. When I was able to, I repaid him the best way I knew how: by being the good son; by being generous to him and to my mother; and by trying to earn his respect. In the end, I like to think that I succeeded.

As I sat solemnly on a memorial bench near the gravesite, the once sunny Florida sky started to darken, churn, and boil into an angry, gray swirl. I heard several loud thunderclaps in the distance, and then a quiet hush fell over the beautifully manicured landscape. A light rain started to fall. Looking around at the perfectly lined crosses, I thought about D-Day, and when my dad visited his friend's grave above Omaha Beach. Now it was my turn to be overwhelmed by the moment, by thoughts of a life just ended, and I decided it was time for me to go. It was also time for my father's story to be told, and after a last touch of my finger tips to his cold, damp grave stone, I decided to do just that.

*"Every man who stepped foot on Omaha Beach that day was a hero."*

**General Omar N. Bradley**

**General Eisenhower's D-Day Message to the Allied Forces**

SUPREME HEADQUARTERS
ALLIED EXPEDITIONARY FORCE

Soldiers, Sailors and Airmen of the Allied Expeditionary Force!

You are about to embark upon the Great Crusade, toward which we have striven these many months. The eyes of the world are upon you. The hopes and prayers of liberty-loving people everywhere march with you. In company with our brave Allies and brothers-in-arms on other Fronts, you will bring about the destruction of the German war machine, the elimination of Nazi tyranny over the oppressed peoples of Europe, and security for ourselves in a free world.

Your task will not be an easy one. Your enemy is well trained, well equipped and battle-hardened. He will fight savagely.

But this is the year 1944! Much has happened since the Nazi triumphs of 1940-41. The United Nations have inflicted upon the Germans great defeats, in open battle, man-to-man. Our air offensive has seriously reduced their strength in the air and their capacity to wage war on the ground. Our Home Fronts have given us an overwhelming superiority in weapons and munitions of war, and placed at our disposal great reserves of trained fighting men. The tide has turned! The free men of the world are marching together to Victory!

I have full confidence in your courage, devotion to duty and skill in battle. We will accept nothing less than full Victory!

Good Luck! And let us all beseech the blessing of Almighty God upon this great and noble undertaking.

Dwight D. Eisenhower

## Official Roster of the 7th Naval Beach Battalion, Company B-6, 11 February, 1944

SEVENTH BEACH BATTALION
11 February, 1944
Co. B-6

| | | |
|---|---|---|
| ANDERSON, C. H. | Lieutenant | Beach Master |
| HALL, F. M. | Lieutenant, Jg | Medical Officer |
| RIVERS, T. E. | Lieutenant, Jg | Executive Officer |

HYDROGRAPHIC SECTION

| | | |
|---|---|---|
| BLIZZARD, J. H. | 812 22 18 | BM2C |
| HIGHLANDER, L. V. | 828 35 44 | S2C |
| McCLAIN, JOSEPH | 575 86 65 | S2C |
| McCLURE, GORDON | 893 12 63 | S2C |
| POULTON, JOHN, Jr. | 761 92 48 | S2C |
| PRIMET, E. J. | 377 81 70 | S2C |
| REEVES, R. P. | 837 41 54 | S2C |
| SCHULTZ, L. L. | 204 72 02 | S2C |
| SHIRLEY, A. A. | 829 60 00 | S2C |
| SMITH, S. F. | 926 99 26 | S2C |
| STANFORD, L. A. | 800 54 43 | S2C |
| STANLEY, E. W. | 653 30 03 | S1C |
| STEMPKOWSKI, E. J. | 822 60 25 | S2C |
| STORRS, N. G. | 820 68 82 | S2C |
| SULLIVAN, W. E. | 233 93 03 | S2C |
| SWISTRO, T. M. | 825 21 16 | S2C |
| TARASKAS, JOSEPH | 817 99 02 | S2C |
| THERRE, A. H. | 800 61 09 | S2C |
| TOMLINSON, P. W. | 653 94 62 | S2C |

BOAT REPAIR SECTION

| | | |
|---|---|---|
| BROWN, R. C. | 862 34 83 | CM2C |
| DAVIS W. H. | 884 87 50 | EM3C |
| EDDY, I. E. | 627 62 26 | MOMM1C |
| HANSEN, A. O. | 654 48 25 | SF2C |
| HORN, R. W. | 822 95 45 | MOMM3C |
| HOUSE, F. L. | 608 88 43 | MOMM3C |
| KISKO, J. P. | 811 50 52 | CM3C |
| LANGENDORF, D. D. | 377 88 97 | SF3C |

COMMUNICATION SECTION

| | | |
|---|---|---|
| DEMSKEY, S. | 810 69 16 | S2C |
| DICKELMAN, E. M. | 851 80 43 | S2C (RM) |
| DUBE, G. H. | 208 96 48 | S1C |
| HEVRIN, E. F. | 726 66 15 | S2C |
| HORNBURGER, T. | 863 83 29 | S2C (SM) |
| THOMPSON, E. | 810 68 29 | S1C (RM) |
| WICKERS, J. D. | 809 45 86 | S1C (RM) |
| YARNUTOSKI, A. J. | 809 64 72 | S1C |

MEDICAL SECTION

| | | |
|---|---|---|
| CARHUFF, J. R. | 647 60 88 | PHM3C |
| HORAK, G. F. | 826 66 65 | PHM3C |
| LAMOTHE, J. H. | 643 09 44 | HA2C |
| LOGAN, R. E. | 570 22 71 | HA2C |
| MAHAN, D. P. | 841 17 56 | HA2C |
| McKEE, A. B. | 809 61 48 | HA2C |
| MELBYE, R. W. | 610 72 58 | PHM2C |
| WALDREP, H. M. | 724 15 75 | HA2C |

**President Truman's Message to those who served in World War II**

Gilbert Henry Dube

*To you who answered the call of your country and served in its Armed Forces to bring about the total defeat of the enemy, I extend the heartfelt thanks of a grateful Nation. As one of the Nation's finest, you undertook the most severe task one can be called upon to perform. Because you demonstrated the fortitude, resourcefulness and calm judgment necessary to carry out that task, we now look to you for leadership and example in further exalting our country in peace.*

Harry Truman

THE WHITE HOUSE

Gilbert H. Dube, USN
May 11, 1925 – February 22, 2003

**Medals and Citations Earned by Gilbert H. Dube, USN**
(reading from left to right)

**Service Issues**

- Presidential Unit Citation
- American Campaign
- European/African/Middle Eastern Campaign

---

- Asiatic Pacific Campaign
- World War II Victory
- French Croix de Guerre with Palm

**Commemorative Issues**

- World War II D-Day
- Overseas Combat Service
- Victory In Europe

---

- Asiatic Pacific Victory
- World War II Victory
- U.S. Navy Service

## Bibliography and Recommended Reading


1. Bacon, Garwood. “D-Day: Soldiers Stories.” Available from http://www.military.com/Content/MoreContent1/?file=dday_0044p1. Internet; accessed 14 January 2004.

2. Davey, Kenneth C. “Sailors Dressed Like Soldiers,” Naval History Magazine, October 1999. Also available from http://www.usni.org/navalhistory/articles99/nhdavey.htm, Internet; accessed 11 January 2004.

3. Dictionary of American Naval Fighting Ships. “Scania.” Available from http://www.hazegray.org/danfs/amphib/aka40.htm. Internet; accessed 10 January 2004.

4. Dube, Gilbert H. “Memoir of My World War II Experiences,“ Unpublished manuscript, 1999.

5. Exercise Tiger, Naval Historical Center. Available from http://www.history.navy.mil/faqs/faq20-1.htm. Internet; accessed 15 January 2004.

6. Gawne, Jonathan. *Spearheading D-Day: American Special Units in Normandy* (Paris: Histoire & Collections, 1998), pps. 226 - 241.

7. Historical Section, COMNAVEU. "Administrative History of U.S. Naval Forces in Europe, 1940-1946." vol. 5. (London, 1946), pps. 301 – 337. Also available from http://www.ibiblio.org/hyperwar/USN/rep/Normandy/ComNavEu/ComNavEu-563.html and http://www.ibiblio.org/hyperwar/USN/rep/Normandy/ComNavEu/ComNavEu-507.html. Internet; accessed 10 January 2004.

8. Kruh, David. “A Brief History of Scollay Square: Sally Keith, Queen of the Tassels”. Available from http://www.bambinomusical.com/Scollay/Interview.htm. Internet; accessed 14 January 2004.

9. Nesbitt, William R. Jr., M.D. “Lessons from D-Day,“ Physician Magazine, May/June 2000. Also available from http://www.family.org/physmag/missions/a0011568.html. Internet; accessed 13 January 2004.

10. Prados, Edward F. (ed.). *Neptunus Rex: Naval Stories of the Normandy Invasion* (Novato, CA: Presidio Press, 1998), pps. 165 - 228.

11. Rhodes, George. "Normandy Remembered," Attleboro Sun Chronicle, 6 June1999, pps. 1, 8.

12. Saving Private Ryan Online Encyclopedia. "7th Naval Beach Battalion." Available from http://www.sproe.com/S/s-7thnbb.htm. Internet; accessed 9 January 2004.

13. Shoulars, Julius (ed.). "History of the U.S. 7th Naval Beach Battalion." Available from http://www.4thbeachbattalion.com/7th_NBB_History.htm. Internet; accessed 9 January 2004.

14. Strictly GI, Testimony (Omaha Beach - D-DAY - June 1944). Available from http://users.skynet.be/jeeper/page85.html and http://users.skynet.be/jeeper/page92.html. Internet; accessed 10 January 2004.

15. Trevett, Jason. "D-Day Beach Battalions Honored." Available from http://www.news.navy.mil/search/display.asp?story_id=8530. Internet; accessed 14 January 2004.

16. War Department General Orders, Omaha Beachhead Unit Citations, 15 September 1945. Available from http://www.army.mil/cmh-pg/books/wwii/100-11/ann1.htm. Internet; accessed 14 January 2004.

www.ingramcontent.com/pod-product-compliance
Ingram Content Group UK Ltd.
Pitfield, Milton Keynes, MK11 3LW, UK
UKHW041904190726
13854UKWH00003B/1078